It's All

Good

TIMES AND EVENTS
I'D NEVER
WANT TO CHANGE

CHARLES SACCHETTI

To my dear wife, Luann, who takes care of the family and is always last on her list of priorities.

Foreword

The following stories are true. To all of those mentioned, both living and deceased, you were the major ingredients that allowed this book's recipe to come together to form a tasty tidbit that is created with love, great memories and gratitude.

The old man hobbled over to his favorite park bench. His knee was throbbing from the arthritis he had learned to live with and accept as his steady companion. As he took a deep breath, to help the pain subside, he noticed a group of boys playing a pickup game of baseball. The batter hit a sharp grounder to the shortstop who missed it for an error. The old man thought, "That's a play I would have made."

Table of Contents

1

Getting in the Game

BACK IN 1955, I decided that I wanted to be a baseball player. My dad had taken me to my first Phillies game, at Connie Mack Stadium, and I was completely enthralled by the smell of the grass and pure beauty of the game. It was with these thoughts in mind that I joined my first baseball team, the Southwest Colts just before my 8th birthday.

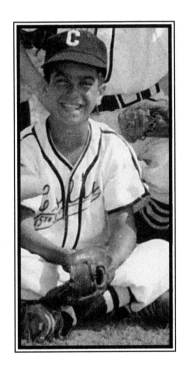

Back then, things were different. Teams played to win and actually kept score! There were no trophies for just showing up, you had to earn them, either individually or by your team winning the championship. Every kid didn't get to play. You had to beat out the other guy. Being the youngest and smallest kid on the team, my position was "bench". The Colts ended up undefeated that year. The coach, Charlie D'Amico, played the guys he thought were the best. I couldn't break into the lineup, it was very frustrating. After each game, as my dad arrived from work he'd ask me two questions:

Did you win?
Did you play?

My answers would be yes and no and always in that order. Dad wouldn't say much more, obviously feeling that I was now old enough to deal with adversity. I really wanted to show him that I was good enough to play but the disappointment continued.

Then one afternoon, as I occupied my usual position while doing my best to avoid the splinters, a few tears began to flow as I realized that I'd have to again go home and give Dad my yes and no answers. My dismay turned to horror when I saw my mother talking to our coach. This is a no no. No kid wants "Mommy" interceding for him, especially at the tender age of 8. However, the next thing I knew, the coach said to me, "Grab a bat; you're pinch hitting." It seems Mom had "reasoned" with the coach, just about begging him to give me a chance.

I now can look back and realize that from that moment, my life probably took a major turn.

I went to the plate with Mom, my older teammates and the coach watching intently and lined the first pitch right through the middle for a single. I felt like I just won the World Series, although I acted like it was no big deal. It was very important to be cool at the age of 8 when the other guys on the team are 11 and 12. I finished that first year 6 for 13, playing sparingly but at least I could tell Dad I played.

From then on, I went on to play for many teams, among them John Bartram High School, Roche Post American Legion, Temple University and a brief stint with the Phillies Organization, shortened by active duty with the National Guard during the Viet Nam War. I say with as much modesty that I can muster that my baseball career was filled with many individual and team honors.

In April of 1970, while on the firing range at Ft. Leonard Wood, Missouri, I received a letter from Temple Athletic Department icon, Al Shrier. Al offered me the position of Business Manager of Athletics which I assumed in August. Two years later, I moved on to the Facilities Department. My boss was Bud Wilson, the brother of my baseball coach, Skip Wilson. During this time, I met a sweet young lady. She was a student, the daughter of my co-worker, Rose. That sweet young lady and I were married two years later. That was 42 years ago. Now there are two children and two grandchildren.

Back in 1955, it would have been easy for me to sour on the game, especially after "failing" all of those times, suffering the humiliation of underachieving. Who knows, I may have even given up the game. It certainly wasn't any fun and I sure didn't like telling Dad I was a benchwarmer.

It was Mom grabbing the coach and pleading with him to give her little boy a chance that made me realize I could play and be successful. As you can see, the most important events of my life had a connection to my playing baseball.

One can never know the consequences of a mother's act of love.

2

After the Pasta

IN MY NEIGHBORHOOD, Italian-American families had many traditions. To mention a few, Christmas Eve always included a seafood meal called the feast of the 7 fishes, plastic slipcovers adorned the furniture in every living room and Sundays always started with mass followed by Mom frying meatballs and sausage while making the gravy (not sauce).

That wonderful creation would simmer for several hours before its marriage to some type of pasta for the Sunday meal.

After the meal, came another tradition. In our family, my father, his brothers and my grandfather would meet at one of their homes and spend 3 hours in intense battle. No physical violence was involved of course, besides, after a meal like that, no one had the inclination toward physical activity. The battle to which I refer was the weekly card game. As a young boy, the card game was a treat for me to watch. I enjoyed watching them play cards as much as I enjoyed watching TV.

No one played for money. It was strictly for bragging rights. All of the brothers had nicknames. Uncle Fred was "Woodpecker", Uncle Mario was "Slats", Uncle Joe was "Joe Pierre" and my father, Henry was "Riggie." Although grown men, no one would dare call Grand Pop anything but "Pop". It would be unheard of for any of the sons to call him by his first name. Thankfully, to this day, that type of "enlightenment" has never invaded our family. He was their father; therefore he was always treated with honor.

They usually started by playing a few Italian warm-up games, like "briscola" or "scopa". After an hour or so, they got down to business....Pinochle. Uncle Mario was clearly the best player. In fact, he made daily bus trips to the casino, well into his 80's, to play poker. He more than held his own. The youngest brother, he would always be teamed with Grand Pop. My father, the oldest son, would be teamed with Fred or Joe. They alternated since my father had seniority! Back in the 50's no one had air conditioning. We had fans and in the summer months the windows and screen doors were always open. After each pinochle hand was completed, the players would "critique" one another's performance. No one critiqued Grand Pop, for the reasons mentioned above; however everyone else was fair game. This was the part I liked the most. They would yell and call each other names in Italian. I would do my best to write them down, for future use on my buddies but I had trouble spelling them and they came too rapidly for me to keep up! With elevated voices, they loved to offer unsolicited opinions on each other's decisions and intelligence levels. With the windows open, the neighbors were used to the noise but any strangers walking outside for a Sunday stroll didn't know whether they should just walk faster or call the cops to report a riot. The interesting thing was that these post mortems only lasted a minute or so and then the next hand would begin. There was never a verbal carryover from the previous hand. Once the new hand begun, the slate was wiped clean…until that hand was over.

I have come to realize that I learned a lot from watching those games some 60 years ago. I learned that it was ok to be competitive and passionate about winning. This really helped me during my baseball and sales careers. I learned to appreciate the camaraderie between men which I now hold as one of my most treasured gifts. And finally, I learned something even more important. When the card game ended those men, who just minutes before acted like they were ready to kill each other, would get up from the table to hug and kiss each other and say goodbye.

That showed me that love of family trumps everything.

P-52927

3

Getting the Message

IN THE SPRING of 1957, for some inexplicable reason our father, Henry Sacchetti, decided that we should see how he made his living. Dad worked at the Westinghouse Electric Corp., at the Lester, PA plant. Many Southwest Philly men did the same, with many others working at the General Electric facility at 67th and Elmwood Ave. Being 10 years old with a teenage sister, I knew some things about Dad's job but I was too busy being a kid to care a whole lot.

Dad never really talked much about his job. I'd see him at the dinner table with nicks, burns and various cuts on his hands and arms. I knew he couldn't hear very well. On a couple of occasions, I overheard him tell Mom about a co-worker who "dropped dead" while at his work station in the "Blade/ Hammer Shop". I knew he never missed a day's work. It didn't matter if he was sick, he went in anyway. There was that Friday afternoon, when I was about 4 years old, that Dad had one-half of his pinky finger chopped off when his machine malfunctioned. Lawsuit? Big Cash Settlement? No, Dad's re- action was to report to work, as usual, the following Monday morning. His 1957 Dodge Coronet didn't have air condition- ing (or power steering!) so he always looked hot when he came in, even if it wasn't hot outside. As I think of these things now, they were kind of strange but heck, I was just a kid more concerned about Richie Ashburn's batting average than what my Dad did for a living.

So, we were told that Mom, Kathy and I would have the privilege of attending "Family Day" on Saturday at the Westinghouse Plant in Lester. We knew little else except that we would be able to actually see what Dad did to keep us fed, clothed, healthy and warm on those cold winter nights.

After a brief welcome from some guy in a suit, the tour started. I remember walking up two flights of metal stairs and down a long corridor. I noticed the more we walked, the warmer it became.

Then it happened.

We walked through a heavy metal door onto a catwalk that was suspended about 20 feet above the work area. I looked down at the floor and saw what I could only describe as an inferno. My 15 year old sister Kathy said, "Oh my God, we're in hell." The guide said the temperature was about 110 degrees on the shop floor.

The shop consisted of numerous furnaces, flames a blazing. Some of my Dad's coworkers were actually working that day and we could see them using long tongs while holding white-hot steel blades over the flames to "soften" them up. The men then would place the blades under the huge hammer, which came down, repeatedly, with a deafening bang. The hammer shaped the blades to spec. These blades would become part of turbine engines, many of which were used by the military during WW II. The post war era had provided new uses for industry.

So now we knew exactly what Dad did for a living.

After the tour was over on the way to the car, Dad took me aside and said…."This is the kind of work you have to do when you don't have an education." At that moment, I made a conscious decision to do well in school so I wouldn't have to have a job like this.

As I grew up I came to appreciate the sacrifice Dad made for us. The oldest of 6 children, he had to quit school and go to work, to help the family. With only an 8th grade education, he was my "human dictionary" while I was in college. He was an extremely bright man in many ways. Circumstances led him to Westinghouse and he worked at that job for 41 years. He was able to enjoy a long retirement and died a beloved Pop-Pop at the wonderful age of 91.

Dad made sure I got the message on that Saturday in 1957. And I can't thank him enough.

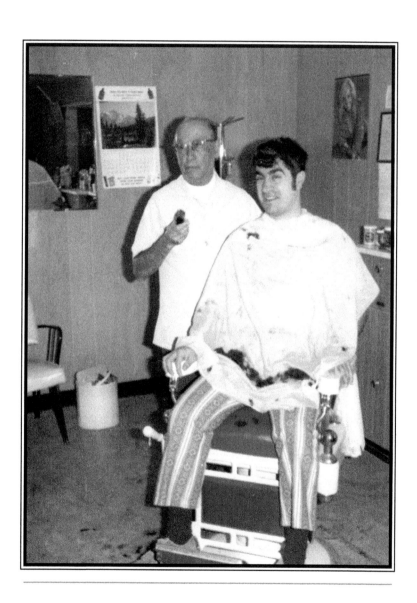

4

The Maestro's Touch

IN THE 50'S, as a kid growing up in my Southwest Philly neighborhood, I like many other's knew where I would spend about an hour or so every third Saturday morning. That would be sitting in one of about 10 chairs, while waiting to get a haircut from the one and only Chris Arcadi. Chris owned and operated his barber shop at the corner of 65th and Buist Ave. Back in those days, few 10 year old kids would dare wear his hair long. It was a crew cut or be prepared to suffer the consequences that would start as soon as you left the shop. Three or four of your best crew-cutted pals would stand in ambush to launch an attack, messing up your hair while yelling the dreaded term, "swats".

It was common for Chris to have the shop full of kids from 8 a.m. to noon every Saturday. Our block contained about 70 homes as did the adjoining streets. Being a mostly Irish and Italian Catholic neighborhood, these homes provided lots of youthful mush-filled heads that needed to be pampered. Saturday was the big day. Chris was a master of the automatic clipper. He would attach a plastic crew cut gizmo onto the clipper and away he went. Once you made it to the barber chair, he could finish the job in about 15 minutes. He was like an Italian Leonard Bernstein, in full command orchestrating the thing he did best in the world.

Now Chris was also a skilled hair stylist. Once we all got a little older and realized that girls were not just put on this earth to be the target of snowballs, we availed ourselves of his artistry. And so it was for me, seeing Chris on a regular basis throughout high school, college and beyond. He and I had a special relationship and had some remarkably deep conversations in the 30 minutes or so it took to cut my hair. Once he found out that I was taking Spanish in High School, he would spend 10 of our minutes speaking Spanish to me with the hope that I would benefit from his multi-lingual language skills. Nice try Amigo. Some of us are preordained to struggle with only one language.

As the 70's rolled around, Chris was elderly and not in the best of health. He decided to take a big step, sell the business he loved for so many years and retire. This would be doubly difficult because his shop was located on the ground floor of his home. His sweet wife, Rose, operated a dress shop that had an adjoining door to the barber shop. So Chris might be "gone" from his business but he wouldn't be gone. The sale happened and almost immediately he regretted it. I lived right across the street and I would see him on his front step seeing all of his customers entering and exiting the shop. He wasn't regretful because of the loss of income; he missed the banter with his buddies and seeing all of the new flock of little kids that took our place. Most of all, he was sad that he was deprived from doing the one thing he loved the most.

I had found a new barber whom I visited twice. Not bad but he only spoke English! I missed Chris too. As I sat with him on his steps, one afternoon, I suggested he become semi-retired and pick up one customer. There was an "understanding" that

Chris would not suddenly decide to work again and compete with the new owner. That was fair. This new guy had to protect his investment. However, since Chris was like family, I saw no harm in his cutting my hair in his home. And he did...for about 4 more years and then his health really started to deteriorate.

By now I was out in the working world and I must say that I was a bit concerned about Chris' health. I was equally concerned with my potential danger given the fact he was getting quite forgetful. It wouldn't be good if he forgot what that straight razor was for! I had grown to be quite fond of my ears. However, when I would sit down in his kitchen chair for my haircut, it was like an automatic pilot kicked in. He still cut hair flawlessly. The Maestro still had his touch.

About a year later, with Chris now well into his 80's and continuing his journey, I became engaged to my wife. When I told Chris the first words out of his mouth were, "I promise, Imma gonna givva you da best haircut you ever had for da wedding." At that point, given the enormity of this haircut, one may have had second thoughts and seek out a hot shot center city stylist to assure success. I wasn't surprised at Chris' promise and didn't hesitate at all to tell him I would be honored. In my neighborhood, my friends and I were raised to value loyalty and there was no way anybody else would touch this noggin once Chris made that remark. Anyway, I figured that my wife was so beautiful that no one would be looking at me.

So, on Friday, May 30, 1975, the day before our wedding, I walked up Chris' front steps and was greeted by a big hug from Rose. We walked into the kitchen, with the fragrance of peppers and eggs in the air. The Maestro put on his smock and proceeded to give me a haircut that lasted a good hour. It was flawless. People did notice and I actually received a few "thumbs up" from my buddies.

Not long after Chris passed away. Thinking of him now, some 40 years later and realizing the blessing he was, I can still see him, clipper in his hand, talking to the kids, unlit cigar in his mouth, keeping that Saturday morning assembly line moving on and on.

5

The Ultimate Sneaker

IT IS SAFE to say that there were very few, if any, people in my neighborhood that you would call "bluebloods". Very few dukes and earls worked in the factories of Westinghouse and General Electric, the two largest employers in our area. What my neighborhood did have, however, were hundreds of hard working, honest and moral men who carried their lunch buckets each day and gave 100 % to the jobs that allowed these men to take care of their families. When I was a kid, in the 50's, things were different. Mother's rarely went out of the home to work. They were too busy taking care of the kids and running the everyday business of the home. These women generally did a wonderful job and I'm proud to say that my mother was one of them.

Like most factory workers, my dad never made a lot of money. At the Westinghouse, Lester P.A. plant, he was a member of the Electrical Union and wages depended on the current terms of the contract. Back in those days, like now, salaries were never quite enough to put one on "easy street". Therefore, it was incumbent upon Mom to make sure the dollars stretched.

And she sure could do that.

I remember her buying Welch's grape juice. Mom realized that drinks like lemonade and grape aide were part juice, part water. So she cut out the middle man and mixed 1 part water with 4 parts Welch's and ended up getting 25% more volume of a tastier drink as compared to the others. I must confess, however, on the QT I would pour a few ounces of the high test into a cup and enjoy the juice as nature intended it.

Mom always knew which stores had the best prices for the different items she needed. Vic's Cold Cuts on 64th and Buist Ave. was the place to go for lunchmeat. Vic's wife ran the place and was a true believer in her products. The rolls of Genoa salami, ham, and provolone were no match for the slicer and her quick hands. The best part of the slicing process would be when she would help herself to a fresh piece of salami and give you one too. No doubt this practice was done only in the interest of "quality control"!

The Acme on 65th and Elmwood was the best supermarket, while Al's was the butcher of choice at 64th and Dicks Ave. Now it must be noted that Mom didn't drive. So she had to walk to all of these places and carry the bags while we were at school. She and the other mothers were happy to make that sacrifice to assure the best values for their families. So, knowing the frugality of dear Mom, it was with some trepidation that at the age of 12, I approached her with an idea.

I was a kid that was always outside playing sports. Day in day out, if I had the chance outside I would be. And, like most kids my age, I was very tough on footwear, especially sneakers. Mom would buy me a pair of PF-Flyers or the like and they would last me about 3 weeks before my big toe saw daylight! About this time, I became aware of the sneaker of all sneakers....

Converse All-Stars, the Chuck Taylor model.

Aside from looking great, they were reputed to wear like iron and help you to perform to your athletic pinnacle. Every NBA basketball player wore them as did just about every college player. They were simply the best. I knew I would have to overcome one big hurdle if I were to be successful in having Mom to agree to buy me a pair:

PF-Flyers cost about $3.00, Converse cost almost $9.00.

After being extra sweet for about 1 week and getting into no trouble whatsoever, I decided to deliver my proposal after giving Mom a big hug and telling her how much I loved her. She knew something was up but that little Sicilian smile told me I had a shot. I promised her that the Converse would last me at least 6 months because of their superior workmanship I vowed to take extra good care of them. No running in puddles or tree climbing etc. Then I mentioned the clincher.

My neighbor, across the street, was the manager of the South Philadelphia Boys Club, at Broad St. and Oregon Ave. He had a contact at a large sporting goods store on Spring Garden St. in center city and could arrange for us to get a discount for the sneakers and pay $7.25 instead of $9.00. All of my points were well received and Mom said yes.

The next part of the story I have shared with my kids and hold as one of the greatest examples of how a parent can teach her kid a valuable lesson while showing sacrifice and love.

On a very hot August day, Mom and I hopped on the 36 trolley car to City Hall and walked the 8 blocks to the store on Spring Garden St. The total trolley fare for both of us was $.88. I got my sneakers. Including the trolley fare, we saved about 90 cents on the transaction. What did I learn as a 12 year old? I learned that if you can present your case in a way that makes sense, you have a good chance of prevailing. I learned that even limited funds can be spent if the cost can be justified. And lastly, I learned that seeing the smile on my face was worth a lot more to Mom than the 90 cents.

6

A Love Tap Well Deserved

GROWING UP IN a strict Italian-American family was never dull though quite predictable. My father, who was most certainly the head of the clan, had few rules that were explained with fanfare but my sister, Kathy and I clearly understood what was expected of us by the way he led by example. Of all the things Dad imparted to us, I would say the importance of a good work ethic and the absolute need to show respect to others, stand out in my mind.

Regarding being respectful, I learned a valuable lesson in less than 10 seconds one day when I was 13 yrs old. It was a beautiful fall afternoon and I was engrossed in a hotly contested two-hand touch football game at our "Coliseum" otherwise known as the St. Barnabas schoolyard on 64th st. in Southwest Philly. As I glanced at my watch, I noticed the time was 4:58 p.m. That time was significant when you take into account that one of Dad's strictest rules, simply stated, was that **dinner was at 5:00 p.m. and don't be late**. Dad arrived home from his job at Westinghouse about 4:30 daily. Mom always was sure to have the meal prepared, so Dad wouldn't have to wait too long for the nourishment he needed for the physically demanding factory job he endured for many years.

We had a typical row home on 64th and Buist Ave. It was comfortable enough although the kitchen was somewhat cramped. Because of this, Mom's chair would always be pushed to the side, while she was cooking, because when it was in her place at the table, she would not have enough room to stand at the stove. Therefore, out of respect for my Mother's laboring in the hot kitchen, it was always my job to make sure that I placed Mom's chair in its rightful dining spot, at the table, before I myself sat down to eat.

So when I glanced at my watch and saw the dreaded 4:58, I knew for me this game was over and I'd better hustle home, one block away. As I ran into the house, I could see that Dad and Kathy were already seated and Mom was just finishing up. Dad had already started with the Escarole soup, with the little meatballs. Rather than getting Mom's chair, I went right to my seat, sliding past her chair, like Fred Astaire on the dance floor. I was in a hurry and I was hungry. As I sat down,

Dad said to me, "Where's Mommy's chair". In life, sometimes we say things that we wish we could somehow immediately pull back into our mouths. That's what I did when I uttered the fateful words, "Oh, she can get it herself". My father, while not missing a single stroke of his soup spoon, and with the skill of a conductor waving his baton, grabbed the blade of his favorite bread knife and popped me on the head with the black wooden handle with the three gold dots. No words were necessary. I immediately got up, went over to Mom's chair and placed it in its rightful spot at our dinner table.......and I NEVER forgot the chair again.

In these politically correct days in which we live, I suppose some might call that little love tap harsh treatment. After all, I was just a kid who was hungry and it wasn't a big deal for Mom to just push her chair over there herself. But that wasn't the point. I had disrespected Mom and disrespected Dad. He wanted me to grow up to be a man who deserved respect and that could only happen if I were a man who showed respect.

When I eulogized my Dad at his funeral mass, I recounted this story. Most of the attendees especially my cousins, children of Dad's siblings, laughed and gave nods of familiarity. My cousins weren't surprised a bit. Their parents would have probably done the same thing. Back then, there was simply right and wrong and there wasn't a large grey area like there is today. I ended the story by saying that Dad's reaction at the dinner table only proved that he was a master of "Nonverbal" communication.

Indeed, in those 10 seconds Dad taught me a very clear lesson on respect and how to show it.

7

Don't Mess With Nellie

© City of Philadelphia, Department of Records

BACK IN THE early 60's, growing up in Southwest Philly, Mrs. Nellie Fagan was probably about 70 or so. Mrs. Fagan was a key figure in our lives back then because she owned and operated the soda shop/candy store on 64th and Garman St. This little piece of heaven served as the gathering place of several generations of boys who spent their time playing stickball, chink, wiffle ball and half ball using the store wall as the backstop.

Across the street was St. Barnabas schoolyard. It was a mere trot from Fagan's to enter the world of two hand touch, box ball and handball. So you see we had our own "Sports Multiplex" and it didn't cost us a cent. After we were done playing, we would go into the store to replace our burned up calories. Cokes and Pepsi's were 12 cents then. Three TastyKake chocolate cupcakes were also 12 cents....and they were big enough to fill you up. A TastyKake cherry pie, actually had cherries in it! They cost a dime. Mrs. Fagan had the hand dipped Abbots ice cream too. So you could top off your coke and TastyKake meal with dessert. That ice cream was the real thing. My mother would give me a large empty dish to take to the store and Mrs. Fagan would fill it with butter pecan and cover it with wax paper. It was generally intact after the short walk home except for the time I brought a spoon with me and ate about ¼ of the contents on the way back. That only happened once.

We never really did anything bad in those days. Almost all of the mothers were home with the kids so there were always eyes out there to catch you in the act. If by chance you did mess up, and the word got back to your father and mother, there was hell to pay. What passes for "child abuse" today used to be called discipline back then! The most daring thing we did was to climb on the row house roofs to walk up and down the block and retrieve the plethora of roofed half balls from games played in the block long driveway. The climber would simply throw them to the ground and we'd all pick them up, clean them and put them into use. It was a bonanza from the sky.

Mrs. Fagan was a nice old gal and was happy to have "her boys" lounge around outside and inside the store in the old wooden booths. She stood about 5 feet tall...maybe. She walked slowly and wore her gray hair in what you would probably call a bun. These features and her rounded eyeglasses gave her the perfect look of an elderly storekeeper of the 50's and 60's. My group was probably the 3rd generation of boys that she "raised". No matter the age, all of the boys treated Mrs. Fagan like she was our grandmother. If she needed someone to go on an errand, we'd do it. One hand washed the other. On the rare occasion that the corner got a little too noisy, she would pop her head out of the door and give us "the look". That was usually all that was necessary.

But there was that one time.

Back in those days we actually had police who had a beat. The cops in our neighborhood would drive by in their cars and check out the area periodically. We knew most of the cops and several of my buddies dads were cops so we usually had no problem. However, a rookie officer was assigned to the area and he was obviously anxious to "make his bones." Acting like Dirty Harry, for the first few nights, he would tell us to disperse or keep quiet which we would do for 15 minutes or so and then he'd double back on us. He was becoming a nuisance. Now Mrs. Fagan was no fool. It is not good for business when your clientele's habits are disrupted. So she decided to take the matter into her own hands.

Would she call the District Sergeant to complain about harassment?

Would she file suit with the ACLU?

Would she call the Action News' hot line?

No.

The next time he stopped by, with his veteran partner, to chase us she came out with her broom in hand. She asked him to get out of the car. She walked over to him like Earl Weaver about to argue with an umpire and said in her best grandmotherly voice:

"Who the hell do you think you are coming over here and bothering these kids? These are **my boys.** I want them here and I'll take care of them if they don't behave, just like I have for the last 40 years. Now get out of here before I call the District!"

Dirty Harry didn't know what to do or say. I guess the fact that his more seasoned partner was still in the car bent over laughing didn't exactly give him a whole bunch of confidence. He just got back into the car to prevent an altercation. As he made a U Turn to head down 64th st., his partner looked out of the window and said, "Good evening Mrs. Fagan" to which she replied, "So long Billy".

It's always wise to know the territory. Had Dirty Harry done his homework, he would have known that Billy was one of us, about 20 years earlier!

8

The Rite of Passage

Sorry but I just can't do it! For the last 50 years or so, I can't enjoy my favorite pizza or pasta unless I top it off with crushed red hot pepper.

As I was growing up, I soon learned that my Italian-American family was like most of the others I knew. There was always a place for the long hot peppers in the vegetable garden. And aside from the tasty pleasure they provided (although painful at times) a good hot pepper could be the key ingredient of a story that could be shared with family and friends for years.

I remember one Saturday morning when I was about 13 years old. As I was asleep in the middle bedroom on the second floor of our row house, I was awakened, about 8 a.m. by a gagging, burning, feeling in my throat. With eyes watering up, I thought the house was on fire. Upon further investigation, my frantic search led me to the basement and the narrow door that led to the attached garage. Upon opening it, I saw my father standing at the rear of his Plymouth, with the garage door open, tending to a large frying pan full of boiling olive oil. The frying pan was on a wooden board on the trunk of the car. The pan contained a bunch of his favorite long hot peppers that were crackling loudly. Hot pepper fumes were everywhere and had made their way to my bedroom, providing me with my "wake up call". Dad had a hanky around his nose and mouth that made him look like one of the desperados I saw on the Lone Ranger. I told him I was going to call the sheriff. His tearing eyes and coughing told me he was not amused. Of course, this well conceived plan was to give Mom a break and cook the peppers outside, while she was at the store, so as not to subject her to the fumes. His heart was in the right place.

Then there were the pranks. Dad would routinely seek out the hottest peppers he could find from friends and family. After testing them, he would take a worthy specimen to work at

Westinghouse, where he would insert a piece into the sandwiches of fellow pranksters who had made Dad the brunt on earlier occasions. When the lunch whistle blew he and his friends would break into incontrollable laughter as the victims learned the meaning of "payback".

At John Bartram High, I had a friend who one day bragged that he could eat any hot pepper without flinching. He did have a degree of talent as I witnessed on several occasions. He was good. Then one day, Dad brought home a few peppers that a guy from work had brought in. They were supposed to be from Mexico and Dad said they were even too hot for him. Taking his word for it, I took one to school the next day to confront my bragging buddy, who by now had gained quite a reputation and was starting to get a bit obnoxious. In front of all of the guys at the lunch table, I bet him a dollar that he couldn't eat ½ of the pepper without getting a drink or eating some bread for the entire lunch period. With peer pressure being one of the strongest forces in the nature of dopey high school boys, he accepted the challenge. I handed the pepper to him and he obviously hadn't seen one like it before. Thinking he would outsmart the pepper, he inserted it into his mouth and chewed only once, then swallowed it. With 10 of us screaming, laughing and cheering, his face turned as red as a stop light. His eyes watered profusely and he let out a variety of screams not heard in the lunchroom before or since. However, he made it through the whole period and won the bet. He became a legend that day. I was happy to give him the buck.

Finally, there was Aunt Tillie Cipriano. Tillie, a beautiful lady, had no peer when it came to eating crushed red pepper. Being my wife's aunt, I first saw Tillie in action, about 45 years ago, when we visited her and had dinner at her home in Longport, N.J. As Tillie sat at the table, she grabbed her dish and began to coat the bottom of it with pepper. The entire bottom was covered with about ¼" of pepper. Sitting next to her, I just stared as she added the spaghetti to the dish. Still watching, I surmised she would now mix everything up, along with the gravy she had added.

Nope….she wasn't done yet.

She then coated the top of the entire dish with the same amount of pepper that was on the bottom. I was nearly awe-struck as she began eating her meal and not flinching one bit. I was in the presence of greatness.

I guess I was about 18 when I started to enjoy eating hot peppers. I didn't realize then what I learned later. Like all of the other male members of the family, I now could relate to the stories told by my father and uncles on a different level.

I was proud to have joined the club.

9

Making the Catch

HENRY'S BALL   CHARLIE'S BALL   MIKE'S BALL

OK, I'LL HAVE to admit it. I love family traditions. No matter what they are, I find a great deal of satisfaction and joy in knowing that a certain practice, that has special meaning, will occur like clockwork among those I love. I'm also a lover of the game of baseball. So naturally, if such a tradition involves the game of baseball, that makes it sweeter.

At the age of seven my father, Henry, bought me my first baseball glove, ball and bat. To me, those three gifts were priceless. They allowed me to start to learn how to play the game and my dad was a willing tutor. Soon after, baseball became my passion. I was enthralled while listening to the games on the radio, with Byrum Saam announcing, while rooting for Richie Ashburn and Robin Roberts. Even though the Phillies were bad in the 50's, it didn't dampen my outlook of the game.

It was about this time that my father showed me one of his prized possessions. In 1944, three years before I came along, he went to see the Philadelphia A's play at Shibe Park. As he sat with his buddies, in the grandstand, a foul ball was hit in his direction, bounced off some guy's arm and landed in dad's lap.

Wow, a souvenir baseball!

When Dad let me hold that game ball I thought it was just about the coolest thing in the world. I'd ask permission to see it, from time to time and as I flipped it into the air, I pictured myself being cheered by thousands of fans as I went 4 for 4 and got the winning hit. There are no strikeouts in little boy's fantasies!

The chances of any one person catching an actual game baseball are slim. Usually 8 to 10 dozen balls are used in a big league game. Even if half of them end up in the stands that's only 50 or 60 balls. If there are 25,000 fans attending you can see that a guy doesn't have much of a shot.

So as a 16 year old, when I attended the Phillies-Milwaukee Braves game with two friends on September 6, 1963, I didn't expect to go home with a ball. Joe Montagna, Ron Wagner and I sat behind home plate in the upper deck. The stadium was now named after Connie Mack, the legendary manager of the old A's who had moved to Kansas City in 1954. By the 7th inning, the Phillies hadn't scored a run and it was becoming difficult to stay awake. With the Braves winning 5-0 and their 2nd baseman, Frank Bolling stepping to the plate, I tapped Ron on the shoulder and suggested he go over to 3 cute girls sitting two rows below us and ask their names. He was the logical choice since he was on the aisle and Joe was in the middle. Watching the girls as Ron moved forward, we were all startled by the sound of the ball crashing directly on Ron's vacant seat. The ball went straight up, hit Joe on the head and landed in my arms.

Wow, a souvenir baseball!

Of course, Ron blamed me for preventing him from catching the foul ball and stayed angry at me for a few days. However, he never got to ask the girls their names so if I were the official scorer, I would have had to charge him with 2 errors! On the way home, I realized that both my dad and I had caught game balls at a big league game. Pretty cool! I was eager to tell him and ready for the anticipated "atta boy".

Fast forward to 1971. The Phillies opened their new, state of the art, multi-use facility known as Veteran's stadium. They were quite good during the 70's and those terrible teams of the 50's and most of the 60's were long forgotten. As the Phils continued to play at "the Vet", my wife and I were married and the parents of two small kids. Soon after our son was born, I realized that we had a chance for extraordinary bragging rights. I knew of no one who could claim that 3 generations of men, in the same immediate family, were lucky enough to each catch a ball **during** a major league game. I couldn't wait to tell him that he had the potential to earn family immortality. I explained that all he had to do was catch a ball at the Phillies game. As he dropped his rattle onto his playpen floor, the twinkle in his eye showed me he got the message!

Eighteen years later, on May 19, 2000, my son and daughter arrived at the Vet to see the Phillies take on the Colorado Rockies. As they sat in the 200 level behind 1st base, the Rockie's second baseman Mike Lansing lifted an Andy Ashby fastball down the 1st base line in foul territory. The ball bounced off a seat two rows below my kids and popped into our son's eagerly awaiting hands.

Wow, a souvenir baseball hat-trick!

The story isn't quite over. Our son and his wife, have two young boys. With two boys in the 4th generation, it looks like the odds to keep the tradition alive are looking a lot better.

10

The $500.00 "Bargain"

IN THE FALL of 1969 it was time to make the big move. Being a senior in college and in no way financially well off, I had saved a few bucks and decided to buy my own car. Transportation in general wasn't a problem for me. I had my red Vespa scooter to hop around town and drive to school and I never had an issue borrowing Dad's 1963, 4 door Ford Fairlane 500. But when I saw that ad in the paper I just had to take the plunge.

It read, "1960 Alfa Romeo, maroon convertible. Cream Puff...$500.00"

Then it listed an address of the dealer which I will call Bill's Auto Sales" on Kensington Ave. in Philly. After reading the ad my good sense left me. In its place was the vision of a scene in the classic movie, "the Graduate" with Dustin Hoffman racing down that California highway pursuing Katherine Ross, in his red Alfa convertible to the sound of Simon and Garfunkel singing "Mrs. Robinson." If Dustin could get a girl like that, why not Charlie? Perhaps the Alpha convertible was the missing link!

Poof...back to reality. My father told me I was nuts. There was no way a car like that could sell for only $500.00 unless something was wrong with it. In addition, back in those days, dealers on Kensington Ave weren't exactly poster boys for the Better Business Bureau. Ironically, my Dad was going to buy a new car and he offered to GIVE me his Fairlane, with only 30,000 miles on the odometer, with no strings attached. I told Dad I was very grateful for the offer but let's face it, that type of family car wasn't exactly what this 22 year old was coveting.

He just smiled and walked away.

So, I went to Bill's to check out the car. It looked great, all cleaned up with the top down on this crisp October day. I bought it.

The next day was a little chilly so when I started the car I switched the heater on. No heat, no air flow. I called Bill and

37

he said to bring it back in and he'd take care of it. After 4 days, I called to see what was up? Bill said he had sent it over to his "heater guy" who was the best in the city and was just waiting for him to send the car back. After 3 more days passed I decided to take my Vespa over to talk to Bill and see why the car wasn't ready yet. Upon arrival, I saw the car parked in the same spot at which I left it when I originally returned it for repairs. Bill wasn't there. The gate to his building was locked. Finally after another week he called me and I was able to pick up the car. The heater worked enough that I could feel some warm air. I could live with that.

I drove the car home and parked it in front of the house. The next day, I went outside to start it and got nothing. No noise, no grinding…deadsville. A neighbor checked the battery. It was ok. I had no money to take it to a real mechanic and Bill, the car guy, wouldn't return my calls. I scooted over to Kensington again and he was nowhere to be found. The gate was locked. The car sat in front of the house for 4 weeks. Weeds were sprouting from the dirt that had accumulated under the body. The Little kids on my block kept asking me when I was going to take them for a ride in my "new" car. I detected a snicker or two from the neighbors. Dad never said a word about it.

Mercifully, a girl on my block had a boyfriend who worked on cars who offered to give me $200.00 for it. I was more than happy to make that deal. At least now I didn't have to see it every day when I walked out of the house.

So let's just say I made a mistake and learned a valuable lesson as a young man. This realization was made more apparent by the fact that my buddy's mother, who upon hearing my father was going to trade in his car for a new one, drove directly behind him to the dealer and bought the car immediately. She drove it for 5 more years without a hitch.

My wounded ego was best tended to by my favorite uncle, the beloved Mario, who said to me, "Don't worry about it, this lesson only cost you $300.00 it took me a couple thousand before I wised up."

There was, however, a saving grace to this episode. Several years later, I read in the "Inquirer" that a murder had been committed by a car dealer in Kensington. In fact, Bill was the perp. He was arrested and convicted.

There is nothing like Philadelphia Karma.

11

The Summer of '70

I SHALL NEVER forget the summer of 1970 because I experienced an amazing transformation. In just 120 days, I was changed from a baseball player into a soldier. In April, I was snatched from the well manicured fields at the Phillies baseball complex in Clearwater, Florida and whisked away to the dust and the heat of Fort Leonard Wood, Missouri. Being a member of the Pennsylvania National Guard, the time had come for me to have my basic and advanced training.

I would be a member of ECHO Company, third platoon, a training unit consisting of both National Guardsmen and regular army draftees. Most of the guardsmen were college graduates, in their early 20's, while the draftees were usually about 18 years old. We all went through extensive physical and technical training. It was sometimes grueling but all in all, it was an experience that I enjoyed. Although it's every trainee's obligation to complain about mostly everything, I look back at the experience now and regret that I didn't keep a journal. I met some of the most interesting guys and had some of the best experiences of my life.

For instance, there was Gene, a drafted member of my unit who was only about 2 months from being ordained a Catholic priest and decided it wasn't his proper path in life. He was fine man who must have still had connections with the Lord. It was on the hand grenade course that the grenade he was throwing malfunctioned. The timing mechanism didn't work and the grenade actually activated as soon as he pulled the pin out. However, it didn't explode. It just clicked. The training sergeant standing next to Gene looked like Casper the ghost and Gene simply made the sign of the cross and walked away. The entire platoon was speechless.

Then there was Billy. Billy was a psychology major in college who had a master's degree. He had been drafted a short time after graduation. He was very intelligent and we became very friendly during the first two weeks. One day he told me he was going to get discharged from the army and he knew just how to do it. Billy acted very "gung ho" at first and the drill instructors loved him, so much so that they made him a squad leader. He would bark orders at the troops, be the first one to volunteer to be a demonstrator of new equipment and generally act like he loved soldiering. However, after the first

4 weeks, he started to become withdrawn. His exuberance disappeared and he would just sit in the corner of the barracks at day's end and not talk to anyone. Everyone wondered what was wrong with him. Everyone except Billy and me, that is. I knew just what he was doing. The DI's took the bait and had him set up for some psychological testing. Billy was familiar with all of the tests so he knew just how to act and what answers would most benefit him. After the 7th week of basic training, Billy was given a "General" discharge and he was out. I figured he'd have a good future in politics!

And then there was Noel. This was a young man of 18 who was a draftee from a rural area of Southern Missouri. He was very naive and a nice kid. He looked up to us older guys for guidance and he was having a tough time, especially on the rifle range. You would think that a country boy would naturally be proficient with a rifle but that wasn't the case with Noel. He was the worst marksman in the whole company of over 100 men and was my platoon mate. He demonstrated his lack of prowess daily, for about a week, as we went to the range for practice with the M-16 rifle, the army's newest standard weapon. During "Practice Fire" one soldier would fire and another soldier, his "buddy" would grade him from a rear position. So, each firing lane had two soldiers who would take turns, one firing and one grading. My position was in the firing lane right next to Noel. The lanes were only a few feet apart. I was a good shot so the DI didn't bother with me. He was too busy staying on Noel. You see, the DI's had an ulterior motive. Of course, they wanted the troops to be proficient, in case they were in a combat situation but the other reason was that they bet money on their own platoons. When the day came to "Record Fire", a DI could win or lose a pretty penny depending on the performance of his troops. Because of this, our DI stood over Noel and did his best to "motivate" him to shoot straight. But, it was to no avail. Noel was that bad.

With record fire two days away, I decided to have a little fun. I told my buddy that I was going to shoot Noel's targets instead of mine. The DI wouldn't notice because he wasn't watching me. He was too worried about the guy who would cost him money. Of course, Noel was not aware of my plan. As I lay prone in my lane, the 50 meter targets went up. Boom, I shot down Noel's target. The DI rubbed his eyes in disbelief. "Atta boy Noel, keep it up boy". Noel yelled out "Yippie" Next, the 150 meter target popped up. Blam, I knocked it down. Noel was thrilled. So was the DI. His incessant berating of this kid must have paid off! "Oh boy" he said, no doubt counting his winnings a tad prematurely. Finally, the 300 meter target popped up. That's farther than 3 football fields away. Nonetheless, Bang….down went the target. The DI couldn't believe it. He just hooted and hollered as though he hit the Missouri lottery. As we were lying there, I made every effort to contain myself and not break out into hysterical laughter, especially after this innocent, young, county boy turned his head toward me and said, "Daggone Charlie, I didn't even pull the trigger that time and it went down"!

Of course good ol' Noel messed up record fire. Our DI lost and my buddy and I never said a word to anyone about it. We just took young Noel over to the side and told him he had a bad day and don't worry about it. He didn't.

I knew I should have kept a journal.

12

The Old Switcheroo

IT HAPPENED AGAIN in the spring of 1970. For 4 consecutive years, as spring was just beginning, I mysteriously contracted strep throat. My doctor really didn't know why it was happening. At the age of 22, I still had tonsils and they would get inflamed during the illness but he couldn't say for sure that one had anything to do with the other. So in May of 1970, when I was one and a half months into basic training at Fort Leonard Wood, Mo. I wasn't surprised when I started to get that sore throat feeling that I had grown to expect. Our unit was preparing to go on "Bivouac", a week of maneuvers and other training while living out in the woods with assuredly none of the creature comforts of 6425 Buist Ave. in Southwest Philly.

Everyone said that Bivouac was a real pain, grueling and physically demanding, so I wanted to make sure I would be feeling 100%. We had a few days before we left so I decided to go to "sick call". I thought it would be very easy for me to explain my history to the doctor. In the past, all I needed was a week's worth of penicillin pills and I recovered beautifully. Naturally the doctor would be most appreciative of my helpful self diagnosis and give me the pills in time to pop those babies and be ready to "roll" with my unit. So, at 7 a.m., I went to see the doctor at the infirmary. He was what you would call, "a lifer", a man in his 50's who had spent his entire adult life in the army. When I gave him my background information, he looked at me like a father who had just caught his kid lying about breaking his neighbor's window. And then he said, "I know how you National Guard guys are. I also know bivouac is coming up and I'll bet you're not too anxious to go". With the best look of surprise I could muster, I said "Respectfully sir, I don't mind going on bivouac, I just need some penicillin because I know I'm getting a strep throat". He jammed the tongue depressor in my mouth and said, "You'll be ok. Go back to duty". Nice guy.

Three days later, my throat was killing me. I could barely swallow. We were scheduled to leave for bivouac at 4 the next morning. I knew the only way I would get any relief was to go on "emergency sick call" late at night. The infirmary was closed then and that meant they would take me to the new base hospital and I'd be looked at by one of the younger doctors. Perhaps, I could "reason" with them and get my pills. I figured I could take them while out in the field, tough it out and get better in a few days. Just after midnight, a truck was dispatched to the barracks to take me to the hospital emergency room. As I sat there, another recruit sat next to me and this poor guy really looked sick. I just had a terrible sore throat but this guy looked like he was just run over by a jeep. The room was very busy. An obviously flustered but sweet young nurse came over and put thermometers in our mouths. After a few minutes, she came over and removed them both and laid them on the table. She then was paged and had to answer the phone. The guy next to me fell asleep. I just sat there. I knew I didn't have a fever; I just had a terrible sore throat. When she came back she was distracted again by a patient screaming at her. In all of the confusion, she picked up my thermometer but looked at the other guy, woke him up and said "You're normal; you can go back to the barracks". She then picked up his thermometer and said to me, "You have a 101.4; you'll have to go into the hospital for 4 days".

I DIDN'T HEAR SLEIGH BELLS BUT IT WAS CHRISTMAS IN MAY!

I didn't know this but the base had recently had a meningitis outbreak. The base commander ordered that anyone with a fever over 101 would have to be hospitalized for 4 days rest. I figured that a 4 day stint in the hospital would just about wipe out bivouac and I'd finally get the penicillin I needed. My fate now determined, I went over to the nurse and while straining my voice I told her that the other soldier removed his thermometer while she was away at the phone and his reading may have been inaccurate. She thanked me and said that she would re-take his temperature. I went back, shook him awake and told him to hang in there.

He went back to sleep.

In my third day in the hospital, I was strolling down the corridor and noticed the other soldier talking to the doctor. I gave him the "thumbs up" sign but I don't think he recognized me. After my fourth day, they sent me back to my empty barracks to "rest" until my unit returned. My throat felt much better, the penicillin did its job as I knew it would. The guys returned just in time for the weekend which was Memorial Day weekend. Our entire unit was given a 3 day pass for the holiday. We didn't have "high-fives" in those days but if we did, I would have gotten a bunch of them. It was part of the culture to revere a fellow soldier, who figured out a way to avoid some kind of duty, as long as you didn't hurt anyone. This episode qualified and my buddies and I had a lot of laughs as I shared my story about my week's "vacation" while enjoying our 3 day pass at the Holiday Inn at Rolla, Mo. The town of Rolla will never be confused with Las Vegas but compared to Ft. Leonard Wood, it was like spending a weekend at a resort.

13

A Loving Heart at Christmas Time

IT ALL STARTED in the spring of 1972. One of the perks of my job, in Temple University's Athletic department, involved my using the facilities on a regular basis. This one particular lunch hour, I decided to go out to the tennis courts and practice hitting backhands against the big green wall outside of McGonigle Hall. After about ½ hour, I felt what is best described as a dull ache in my lower back. Over the next few months, the pain worsened and I decided to go to Temple Hospital's Orthopedic Department to find out what, if anything was wrong. After some testing it was determined that I had a herniated or perhaps a ruptured disk, L-5 to be exact. Over the next year or so, my condition worsened and I underwent the usual treatment. That included exercises at first, heat treatments and wearing a back brace during my waking hours.

None of this helped which led to more aggressive treatments. I had two weeks bed rest at home, lying on my mattress that sat on top of a ¾" plywood bed board. I was allowed to get out of bed only to shower and use the bathroom. The bed rest didn't help. I was admitted twice to the hospital for several days of "traction", where weights would hang from my feet to take pressure off of the spine. They didn't help either. Finally, by August of the next year I would try one last thing in an effort to improve my condition and avoid surgery. I would wear a body cast that started at my shoulders and wrapped around my entire torso. The cast was the old fashion kind, plaster of Paris, hot and heavy, especially in August. I wore that cast for a month and then we waited three more to see if there was any improvement. There wasn't.

Running out of patience, I spoke with my doctor and said, "I've had enough of this stuff. Let's get the surgery done." Of course there were no guarantees of success, back in those days there weren't any non invasive laser surgeries. I would have to be cut to have the disk removed. The disk in question was pressing on the sciatic nerve which caused my entire left leg to be completely numb and the pain was a like a toothache that wouldn't go away. The hope was that the surgery would allow the nerve to regenerate over time and healing would take place.

Doctor and patient were now on the same page and I checked into room 939 at Temple Hospital on December 19, 1973. Surgery was set for the 21st. I had an elderly roommate, a Jewish man named David. Dave was in to have a heart valve replacement. Although very common now, this procedure was considered to be quite risky back then. Dave was a wonderful old guy and we talked for hours about our families and how we would pray for each other's successful outcomes. On the 20th, the day before my surgery with Dave still snoozing, I quietly turned on my transistor radio to hear the news and what I heard was shocking. Bobby Darin had just died. He had just had the same surgery Dave was scheduled for and he died from complications. I quickly turned off the radio, thinking that this news was the last thing Ol' Dave needed to hear. Fortunately, Dave was still asleep. Every time a nurse would come in I would tell them not to mention anything about Darin's passing and it was good that Dave didn't like TV. I was able to keep him in the dark.

My parents came to visit that evening. Mom gave me her little statue of the Virgin Mary to keep in the room. That night, Dave asked me about the statue and I explained that we believed Mary could intercede, on our behalf, to her Son, Jesus Christ. Since we believed He was the Son of God, it was a no brainer to ask His mom to help us. Dave had learned that his surgery would also take place the next day. He asked me if I would let him see the statue. I picked it up, gave it a kiss of reverence and handed it to him. Dave, looked at it, smiled and also gave it a little kiss. He then looked at me and said, "I ain't taking any chances."

Thank God, both of our surgeries were successful. I was allowed to go home on Christmas Eve. Dave had to stay in a few days more. When I hugged him goodbye, it felt like I was leaving a good buddy, even though he was old enough to be my grandfather. As I was leaving, he told me he knew about Bobby Darin, after all. The girl bringing in dinner mentioned it to him, while I was napping. He knew I was trying to keep it from him so he didn't want me to feel bad by letting on that he knew.

Talk about a man with a good heart!

14

In Praise of the Secret Service

ON MAY 9TH, 1980, I had the opportunity to have an up close and personal encounter with the Secret Service. I must say that I was greatly impressed.

In October of the previous year, as the Director of Housekeeping at Temple University, I like many others, was very excited to learn that the university would be hosting a "Town Hall" meeting with President Jimmy Carter. This would be unlike anything I previously had to deal with. The world would be watching and the pressure was on to make sure the meeting went off without a hitch on November 5th. That meant that we had about a month to get things in shape. The site of the meeting, McGonigle Hall, would be "spit shined" from top to bottom. New lights would be installed throughout the building. Floors would be polished. Graffiti would be removed. One thousand white folding chairs would be rented to accommodate the invited participants. Special electrical and telephone service would be added. Another building would be set up to accommodate the press. And so on and so on. The Secret Service advance team met with and vetted all of us who would have close contact with the meeting site. My acquaintances and neighbors were questioned about me.

We were ready for November 5th but geopolitics through us a curveball. On Nov. 4th, fifty –two American hostages were taken after Iranian militants took over the American embassy. The town hall meeting was cancelled. President Carter would be too busy trying to get the hostages released and the importance of that town hall meeting paled in comparison.

The White House did, however, promise to reschedule.

In April we were told that the meeting would take place on May 9th. The hostages remained captive but it was an election year and Carter was doing poorly in the job approval category. The economy was bad, mortgage rates were sky high and of course, he was the guy at the top. He was blamed for everything that was bad in the country. In order to help get re-elected he had to regroup and mingle with the folks. The town hall meeting would help him do that.

All of the preparations mentioned above were repeated and May 9th arrived. On Broad Street, across from McGonigle hall, there were hundreds of protestors. They were peaceful but adamant in their displeasure with the president. After we were given our security credentials, several of us were chosen to meet the president and shake his hand so he could express his thanks for our efforts. One of my supervisors was assigned to the press area across the street and she was also chosen to meet the president. I would be given 10 minutes, before the meeting closed, to run across Broad St. and escort her back to the outside patio where we would meet Carter.

When I received the "10 minute warning" I began trotting across the street. Amongst the throng of protestors, I heard someone call me. It was one of my retired supervisors who was just there as a spectator. As he called my name he waived a small camera, obviously beckoning me to take a close-up picture for him. It was no big deal, so I quickly diverted into the crowd to get his little "Instamatic" flash camera. As I turned to resume my mission I felt myself spinning around as two burly guys grabbed me by the arms. I didn't know where they came from but when they said "Secret Service, where are you going" I thought it wise to stop moving, smile and show them my credentials. Then I realized that it's not a good idea to quickly take something from the crowd and run with it when in close proximity to the president.

They let me go after I explained and showed them the camera and I was able to get my supervisor, from the press area and return in time to meet Jimmy Carter as he exited the building. Ironically, almost 30 years later, my son married the daughter of a retired secret service agent, who helped protect George Bush, the elder. When I shared this story with him, he just smiled and was not the least bit surprised.

The whole episode left me with an appreciation of the skills that these agents possess and how they use those skills as they unselfishly protect our top elected officials. May God protect them all.

15

Room 219

THE PRICE OF gold was really high in 1980. Soaring interest rates along with the hostage situation in Iran were fueling fear and uncertainty. As usual, when these kinds of events occur, the value of precious metals usually rises. One of my uncles was a consummate coin collector. He was acutely aware of this axiom and learned to take advantage of it. While on his trips to the casinos in Atlantic City, he would obtain rolls of half dollars and quarters from the cashiers and go through each roll. Back then, there were still silver coins in circulation and also the newer "clads" had a layer of silver in them. These coins were like a "silver sandwich." As the price of gold rose, so did the price of silver. After checking the rolls, my uncle would remove any containing silver. Silver buyers were paying up to 10 times face value for silver coins and somewhat less for the clads, so a smart collector had the potential to make a nice profit.

Back in the real world, my wife and I were married about 5 years, in our first house and our daughter was a cute little one year old who was leading the league in diaper usage. We found out in a hurry that babies could be expensive so we looked for ways to save a buck or make a buck whenever possible. One night I saw an ad, in the Temple Alumni magazine, by the company that provided most of the class rings to the local high schools and colleges. We both had high school rings but neither of us ever wore them. Both rings led a sedentary existence and hadn't moved for years. I checked around and found out that they both contained some gold. How much I didn't know but it really didn't matter. We weren't getting any benefit from them now and we certainly could use the extra cash. We decided to sell them on the open market.

At the northern end of City Line Ave., just before you entered the Schuylkill expressway stood the old Marriott Hotel with the famous Kona Kai restaurant, adjacent and facing the street. I noticed a sign in the window of one of the shops at street level reading, "Precious metals bought and sold." Indeed, it was an upscale jewelry shop, no doubt fancy inside, catering to the well-to-do guests staying at the hotel. I passed the hotel each evening on the way home to Drexel Hill and it would be easy for me to stop there and see what kind of offer our two rings would bring. Meanwhile, on Friday, I saw a small add in the Philadelphia Inquirer, simply stating:

"Buying gold and silver. Top prices paid. Room 219, Marriot Hotel City Line Ave., Friday and Saturday only.

Wow…Talk about good luck; two buyers at the same place. I envisioned a mini bidding war. Saturday, on the way to the hotel I wondered about the best strategy to use. I decided to go into the fancy shop first and then hop up to Room 219 and see what that place would be like.

The hotel jewelry shop was elegant, with artwork, chandeliers and beautiful glass counters that housed all kinds of rings, watches, bracelets and earrings. The somewhat snooty salesman was dressed in a very expensive looking suit which clashed a bit with my jeans and tri colored windbreaker. He gave me sort of a double take and strolled over, obviously thinking I must have walked into the shop by mistake. After I told him I wanted to sell the two rings, he loosened up a bit, asking me to give them to him so he could weigh them and give me a price. He did so and said:

"We'll give you $95.00." I said, "Thanks for your offer, I'll be right back"

I strolled up to Room 219. After I knocked on the door a guy answered who obviously was not an aristocrat. There were papers scattered all over the room. There was some kind of food on a table that I had never seen before and I wondered if it had ever been alive. He had a scale on another small table and there was a scary looking man in a chair looking out of the window; no doubt his security detail. When I told the guy I wanted to sell the two rings he said in badly broken English, "Hokay, give to me".

"Ok buddy here they are."

Then he said the magic number, "$175.00"

"Thanks buddy, I'll be right back"

I went down to the snooty guy and let him know that the man upstairs had offered me $175.00, much more than he did. His condescending response to me was,

"Oh yes but he's a gypsy!

I said, "Maybe so pal, but the "gypsy" is paying green money just like you only there's a lot more of it." "By the way, have you ever thought about becoming a butler?"

I went back to Room 219 and made the deal.

About 8 or 9 years later the hotel closed, allegedly because of too much competition with the center city hotels and management issues. Too bad that "gypsy" was only there for 2 days. He may have been able to help.

16

Uncle Al

IN LIFE, IF you are fortunate enough, you may come upon
a person with whom things just seem to click. For me, one

such person was Alphonse Nocito. Al was my wife's uncle, the husband of Aunt Jeannie, who was the sister of my mother in law. I must admit that when I first heard of Uncle Al, I was a bit intrigued. While dating my wife, I would hear stories about how intimidating he was being a big, tough looking guy that no one dare mess with. Indeed, years later he would share a story with me about an overzealous local politician, who had the bad judgment to try to impose his will on Uncle Al. After this man knocked on the door, Al answered. The intruder was aggressively trying to stick some flyers in Al's face through the half opened door. When Al said he wasn't interested, the guy ignored Al, kept talking and decided to put his foot in the doorway to prevent its closing. Protecting his home from this "breaking and entering" threat, Al popped him in the jaw with a short right. After a brief nap on the lawn, the man decided to move on to the next house. Although a highly intelligent man, who graduated from LaSalle College and had a successful career in the Finance Dept. of the state of New Jersey, stories like this, always overshadowed those of his softer side.

So with great interest and anticipation I looked forward to my first encounter with Uncle Al. It would be at his house during the Christmas holidays in the year 1973. We had been dating for about 7 months and we would accompany her parents for the visit. My girl took great pains to warn me about what I could expect when I met Uncle Al. She lovingly explained that a lot of the family was intimidated by him because he was the epitome of the tough, old fashioned Italian patriarch. She wanted to be sure I wasn't going to be too nervous when we would finally meet. Her introduction didn't go exactly as planned and the look on her face clearly showed it. With only Al and us present, with a smile on my face, I looked him in the eye, shook his hand and said, "You don't look that tough to me, I could probably kick your butt right now!" This was admittedly a calculated risk. Totally surprised, Uncle Al looked at me, furrowed his brow and bellowed a loud laugh as he gave me a bear hug of affection.

That was it. We were buddies for life.

As I got to know him, I would learn of his love of sports, U. S. History and of course, his family. And what a family it was! Uncle Al and Aunt Jeannie increased the population of Delran N.J. by eleven. They brought 6 girls and 5 boys into the world and all of the kids have grown to be outstanding citizens, which speaks volumes of Jeannie's nurturing and Al's strong disciplined leadership. A Korean War vet, Al was also a top flight woodworker. He had a fully equipped basement that allowed him to fabricate many different pieces that would be used in the home. The one I remember the most was the 10' long oak dinner table and the benches that accommodated a typical dinner crowd of 15-20 people.

Some of my best times with Uncle Al were when I would make a "bread run". I had a wonderful Italian bread bakery as a customer, for many years. Whitey, the owner, would not let me leave the bakery unless I took a gift of 2 or 3 bags of rolls with me. Later that evening, I would always bring most of them to Al and Jeannie's. Al was usually, napping in his recliner. I would wake him up and then we would go off to the kitchen to enjoy fresh bread and butter along with Aunt Jeannie's freshly brewed coffee. The laughs and love would fill the room.

Simple pleasures can be ones most treasured.

Al retired in 1993. To supplement his pension, he started his own woodworking business. For years he had dealt with heart problems. Unfortunately, on September 1, 1994, after 39 years of marriage and one year after his retirement, Al passed away. The day after he died, a letter arrived at his home informing him that he had received permission to sell some of his pieces at a prestigious marketplace in New England. One year later, Aunt Jeannie joined her beloved as she also went home to the Lord.

We all hope to leave a legacy. Uncle Al sure did. Aside from his wonderful children and grand children he left a life story that allows his family to sit together and lovingly reminisce.

As for me, he provided some great "guy" time. I think it's called "male bonding" now. Let's just say that sitting at the table with Uncle Al, enjoying a roll with butter and a cup of coffee while talking baseball was a great way to spend an evening.

17

Keeping "In Touch"

ON JUNE 26, 1979, my wife and I were blessed with the birth of our first child, a beautiful little daughter. For me, it was an extra kick because it happened to be my birthday. Naturally, everyone in the family was thrilled with our new addition. She would have 4 loving grandparents to dote over her and shower her with a ton of love. My parents already had two granddaughters, from my sister and her husband, so the birth of our daughter was extra special for my wife's parents, Fred and Rose, who now had their first grandchild.

Rose was a sweet, loving lady who exuded femininity in the fairest sense of the word. She was the ideal mother in law, never butting into our affairs but always there if asked for advice. I joked, while delivering her eulogy, that the only bone I had to pick with her was that she had prevented me from telling "mother in law" jokes because she was so nice. My father in law was a handsome, hard working and gregarious man whose chief loves in life were, God, family and Sinatra… and perhaps not always in that order! He was quite the kidder too. Like her mother, my wife is a meticulous housekeeper but you might be surprised at that if you knew her as a child. She was a holy terror, grabbing everything in sight, knocking things over, jumping on furniture, sliding down the banister and just generally getting into mischief. Dad saw his opportunity for a little good natured "payback". Just about as soon as our daughter was born, he stated his intention to teach her how to run around the house and grab the tablecloth, throw newspapers, and perform other feats of mayhem. At her 1st birthday party, Dad was true to form. He produced a neatly wrapped present and upon opening it we discovered a very realistic looking, toy, hammer He was sure to make a point that it would be put to good use once he was able to teach the baby how to use it.

Three years later on December 19th, our son came along. My wife's pregnancy was a very emotional one since her Dad was engaged in a very courageous battle with lung cancer. Dad died just two months before our son's birth so his arrival was greeted with emotions of every type. Like many great mothers, Rose came to our house in Drexel Hill, Pa. to assist the new mom while she was getting back on her feet after the baby's arrival. After a few days, it was time to take Mom back home to New Jersey. Earlier that morning, I decided to take a walk to the shopping center to pick up a few things. It was about a half mile walk so I had some time to reflect upon the events of the last week and take stock of my new responsibilities now as a father of two. As I walked down State road, towards Lansdowne Avenue, I thought of Fred and said a quick prayer thinking, "Boy Dad, too bad you're not around now. Now you have a boy who could really make use of a hammer."

A few hours later, I loaded up the car with Mom's things to take her home. We started our trip and after about a mile, I drove up the hill just past Garrett Rd. In the distance I saw a fairly large object in the middle of the road that I would have to avoid. As I approached it, my heart skipped a beat and I let out an audible "Whoa", startling Mom. There in the middle of the road was a brand new, shiny, HAMMER...not a plastic toy one, a real one like the kind all men keep in their toolboxes! I kept driving, adrenalin pumping, and told Mom the whole story, from my walk to the store to that very moment. She looked at me in amazement.

Was the hammer in the street a coincidence? I've been driving for over 50 years and I've never seen a hammer in the road. I have unfortunately met up with a nail or two, but never a brand new hammer. Naturally, this story was shared with the entire family the day it occurred and many times thereafter.

Fast forward 24 years. That baby boy is now a young man, contemplating a proposal of marriage to the love of his life. Although sure this is the right thing to do, he has the normal amount of anxiety as he realizes how his life will change forever. Still, the big day arrived and he would pop the question after Sunday mass at the Church of the Sacred Heart, in Riverton, NJ, which incidentally was the site where my wife and I tied the knot. After mass, the young couple strolled into "Mary's Garden", a scenic shrine dedicated to the Blessed Mother. My son's nervousness immediately disappeared when he looked at a nearby bench and saw the shiny HAMMER just sitting there. He then realized that his "Pop-Pop" was giving him the message. "Go for it, kid and don't worry about a thing."

As for me, I have chosen to believe that those hammers were clear examples of Dad's sense of humor that let us know that even though he isn't down here with us, he is still looking out for us and loving his family.

18

An Added Bonus

IN 1993, I made a commitment with the hope of gaining some spiritual benefits and ended up with much more. Our church, St. Charles Borromeo, had just completed construction of the "Perpetual Adoration Chapel". The chapel was built to provide a quiet place where parishioners and guests could go to pray and meditate in the presence of the consecrated Holy Eucharist, which we Catholics believe to be the actual body of Jesus Christ. Since "perpetual" means without interruption, it was the hope of the church that parishioners would volunteer to be "Chapel Guardians" and commit to praying in the chapel one specific hour each and every week of the year, for instance, every Monday from 6:00 a.m. to 7:00 a.m. By doing this, it was hoped that all hour time slots would be filled around the clock, 7 days per week. When the call went out for volunteers I thought it would be a good opportunity, to get more in touch with my spirituality, so I volunteered to be one of the guardians. I was even happier about the decision when my 10 year old son asked if he could join me....quite a commitment for a kid that age.

We had an early Saturday morning time and were joined by a few other parishioners who had made the same commitment, Joe Schofield along with Richie Millilo and his wife Patt. I didn't know them at first but as time went on we naturally spoke before and after our hour and became friendly. As the years passed we found our friendships growing into meaningful relationships that would touch upon all aspects of our lives. We learned about each other's families. We celebrated the good news and comforted each other when misfortune occurred. We gave each other prayers, encouragement and love during illnesses and rejoiced at the weddings of our children.

I had a special relationship with both Joe and Richie. Joe, my son and I would have breakfast every week after chapel time. Joe, who was about 15 years my senior, was like my big brother. He was a self made success, who came from extremely humble beginnings to become a consummate businessman who earned the trust of his clients while guiding their financial decisions. Our breakfast topics ranged from family, sports and world affairs to the economy and the pitfalls of investing in some financial instruments as opposed to others.

I was thrilled to have my boy share this great time with such a good, learned man who was of the highest moral character. Unfortunately, in 2013, Joe became ill and couldn't attend chapel any longer. He eventually passed away in October of 2014.

Richie was a few years older than me and Joe's absence from the chapel only caused us to become closer. He was a South Philly boy who was full of stories about the old neighborhood. He spent years running his family business and now held a very important position with a government contractor. It involved extensive travelling as he regularly met with military officials at the highest level. Richie was also a courageous survivor and did not fear death. He had a life threatening illness for years but always bounced back. He gave thanks to God for his ability to do so and celebrated his good health. His attendance at the chapel was but one way he showed his appreciation. Richie finally succumbed to his illness in June of 2014. I knew that his favorite adult beverage was a gin and tonic. When I visited him, shortly before he died, I just happened to pick up a bottle of gin, some tonic water with enough cups (the nurses provided the ice) to accommodate Richie, his family, my wife, me and our priest friend, Fr. Roberto "Tito" Ignacio. With Richie lucid and smiling, he received the sacrament of the "Anointing of the sick". After the anointing he then sipped (with the doctor's ok) on his favorite drink as we all joined in. The unused gin and tonic were taken home by Richie's daughter, Donna and shared, by the family, as a toast in his honor on the 1st. anniversary of his death.

I continue to attend the chapel at the appointed time. My son, who was married in November of 2007, moved out of the area and worships at his new church. There is at once emptiness but also fullness in the chapel. In my mind's eye I can still see Joe, eyes closed in deep meditation and Richie sitting next to Patt reading from scripture or some other religious piece. The breakfasts that the three of us looked so forward to are no more, Richie no longer shares his "post chapel" cream doughnut and trips to the local yard sales with his beloved Patt. However, the fullness I feel is the knowledge of the wonderful friendship our wives have built with each other. My wife, along with Patt and Joe's wife Rita, have taken up where the guys have left off. And my heart is filled with the wonderful memories of two of my best buddies who just happened to pick the same worship hour that I did. Rather than believe that was just a coincidence, I choose to believe that divine guidance put us there at the same time so that we could share each other's lives while getting a little closer to our Savior.

19

The Return to El Roacho

I REALLY ENJOYED the breakfast sessions with my young son, back in the early 90's. For several years, just about every Saturday after we put in our 1 hour of adoration at Cinnaminson, New Jersey's St. Charles Borromeo church, we would go to one of several local diner/restaurants to eat and usually discuss whatever sport was in season. One place, about ten miles away, was of particular preference to us since it served the best banana walnut pancakes around. In addition, directly next to it was a newsstand that sold various types papers from around the country. We would usually buy "The Sporting News", the bible of professional baseball and discuss several of the stories over breakfast. The kid was very in tuned to sports at this age of 10 or so and his food usually got cold on the plate as it took a back seat to his numerous questions and opinions. Nonetheless, his pancakes always disappeared and the hour or so we spent together made for some great father-son time.

On Sundays, after mass, the whole family usually went out for breakfast. My wife and daughter had their favorite places so we usually accommodated them. They preferred one of many nearby diners on Rte. 130 near our church. Of course the males, in the family, lobbied hard to get them to give our place a shot. Let's face it we had never had a bad meal and it would be good for them to try something different, expand their horizons, so to speak. The girls had no interest in our favorite spot. The Sporting News was not a big selling point to them. They couldn't see the big deal in our loving that place so much. They just wrote it off as being a "guy thing".

It probably took about 6 months or so but finally the girls consented to try our place. As is typical on a Sunday morning, the place was pretty crowded and we had to wait about 15 minutes to be seated. When we first walked into the restaurant, the young hostess looked at us and said. "Oh back again, huh? Looks like you guys can't stay away from here." She obviously was making the point that she had just seen us the day before. Our girls rolled all 4 of their eyes simultaneously. We were seated at a table in the main aisle. My wife sat across from me and our end of the table rested up against a very nice wall beautifully decorated with a country scene. The waitress brought our coffee and the juice for the kids and then left to put in our order. It was at that point that our table for four had a fifth visitor, who was not quite a welcomed guest. An obviously youthful cockroach decided to scale the wall only inches from my wife. As she saw it out of the corner of her eye, she let out a scream worthy of an Alfred Hitchcock movie. She jumped up, grabbed our little girl's hand and ran out of the restaurant. My son and I looked at each other and he said, "Do we have to go too?" After another sip of my delicious coffee we did leave, trying to avoid the quizzical looks that followed us to the door. The manager told me not to worry about paying for the drinks.

Of course, this was all an aberration. Our restaurant was always neat and clean. They couldn't have had a bug problem. That little guy must have been brought in by an outsider or was trapped in a soda carton upon delivery to the restaurant. Of course, this logic was to no avail as I tried to present it to my wife, a lady mind you that was so afraid of bugs that she once called me at my office to let me know one had found his way into our living quarters!

However, the men in the family were not moved by the whole affair. For fun, we dubbed the restaurant "El Roacho" We continued to eat there each Saturday and upon returning home would give the girls a glowing report on both the cuisine and the cleanliness of the facility. In fact, after a month or so, we resumed our lobbying to get the girls to give the place a second chance. We got nowhere.

Then fate stepped in.

My wife's good friend, who was unaware of our story, had mentioned that she and her husband had eaten at the restaurant, had a great time and they had actually become regulars. I saw an opportunity to use this favorable review to give one last pitch for a second chance.

Amazingly, she said yes!

So, the following Sunday, after mass, we made the 10 mile trip to our spot. After walking in and being greeted, I was hit by an idea that came out of nowhere....risky yes but too good to pass up.

I decided to go for it.

As the hostess was escorting us down the main aisle, I started to stomp my feet on the rug as if to be annihilating any critters that may be in the area. We laughed all the way to the table. The other patrons were baffled. The triumphant return to El Roacho was complete.

20

The 15 Year Itch

IN MAY OF 1990, as a sales manager with my company, I was asked to help train a new salesperson in the Hampton Roads area of Virginia, an area that includes Virginia Beach, Norfolk and Newport News. The young lady would have this beautiful area as her "territory" and it was full of great potential. Unfortunately, the time I was needed coincided with our 15th wedding anniversary so that meant I'd be away for that big day but we made plans to celebrate after I returned from my week long trip. We were scheduled to work in the Virginia Beach area on the second day. Although I had been in the Hampton

Roads area while playing ball in college, I had never been to Virginia Beach. The area was beautiful. The beach itself was clean, the concrete "boardwalk" had a brand new bike path, the ocean was lovely and there were a multitude of hotels and restaurants in the area.

I decided to take the family to Virginia Beach for a week vacation in August. Soon after I arrived home, I made the reservations for the trip. We would be staying at the Sheraton Hotel, right on the beach. Out the door and onto the sand... you can't beat that. As the summer progressed, the kids got very excited about the trip. Our kids were 11 and 8 and they, like my wife and I, looked forward to this new adventure. They were especially interested in the travel route, since it would involve taking us over the Chesapeake Bay Bridge Tunnel. This 17 mile long, amazing feat of engineering was something to behold, as it took you both above and under the bay.

Two days before the trip, the radiator in my car sprung a leak and had to be replaced. Thankfully, this happened while we were home and not on the trip so I had no problem taking the car to a local radiator shop to get the job done. In shorts and tee shirt, sitting in the waiting room, I started chatting with Joe, the owner. One thing led to another and when he found out that I sold specialty chemicals, he asked me if I had anything that would kill poison sumac. Being raised in the city, I wasn't familiar with that particular plant but did have a terrible encounter with poison oak one summer. I asked to see the area involved and he took me behind the shop. As I approached the mini jungle, I had trouble seeing the plant so I took a closer look. I checked my product data sheets and determined that our best "weed killer-soil sterilant" would indeed take care of his problem. So, I made the sale which made me happy since it would offset some of the cost of my new radiator.

Win-Win situation....or so I thought.

About an hour later, I started to itch, first my leg, then my arm. I jumped into the shower but it was too late. Blisters were beginning to erupt. By the next morning, I had a bunch of them on both legs, both hands and both arms. They varied in size from tiny to marble size with the largest being on my left knee. I went to the doctor's and she confirmed it was poison sumac.

Although not contagious, the family didn't want to come near me. I was covered with Calamine lotion, gauze pads and tape. I looked like a cast member from the "The Mummy". Of course, I had to have some fun with the situation, so at the right time I would sneak up on my kids and walk toward them, zombie-like, just to hear their squeals as they scurried away.

The trip was still on. If I had to drive the 300 or so miles to Virginia Beach, at least I could control the itch with the medicine the doctor prescribed. The fellow vacationers would just have to get used to my appearance. I engaged in some wishful thinking that things weren't that bad and I would be able to do everything I planned. So to confirm my beliefs, I called my brother in law, a brilliant physician who specializes in infectious diseases.

"I guess the salt water will do the blisters good, right"?

"No, there are bacteria in the water so you best stay out"

"But, at least the sunshine will help dry them up, right"

"No, it will only serve to irritate them. Better keep out of the sun as much as possible. Just keep using the Calamine and keep them dry."

So much for my medical opinions!

However, the trip came off and we made it there ok. I wore shorts and tee shirts every day and had my share of quizzical looks on the bike paths. The biggest saving grace was that that the poison sumac had no adverse affect on my appetite. The first night there we discovered "Captain George's", a fantastic seafood buffet. Nothing makes you forget about a case of poison sumac quicker than a dish of shrimp and scallops along with some hush puppies from the Captain!

We enjoyed the trip so much that we returned to Virginia Beach 3 times. We visited the Captain on the first night of each trip. Those times the only itch in the restaurant, happily, was the "scratch" I needed for the cost of the meals.

21

Bouncing Back

AT THE AGE of 14, he was just about the tallest one of all of his buddies. As a result of this and some natural athletic ability, my son was pretty tough to stop out on the basketball court. He was one of the best performers in our Town League and fully expected to carry that success into high school. In fact, he couldn't wait to start matriculating at his new school and be able to play for its highly respected, veteran basketball coach.

My son had little doubt he'd make the freshman team. Let's face it, he was one of the top scorers and rebounders in town and surely the coach would get a chance to see his skills up close and personal during tryouts over the Thanksgiving weekend in 1997.

Only he didn't take a couple of things into account.

Most of the competitors played CYO ball, which is a league affiliated with Catholic grade schools. The high school was a Catholic school, and the coach had "history" with a lot of these players, having seen them play in league games. My son went to public grade school. Therefore, he was unknown to the coach and his assistants and would have to be really impressive during that short 2 day tryout period to get a good look. Additionally, these kids had played together and many of them had been teammates in grade school. This presented a decided advantage during the scrimmage games played as part of the tryouts. But most importantly, he reported to the tryouts without doing any earlier conditioning program, thinking his ability would certainly compensate for the lack of hard work.

The kid exuded confidence as he left the house on that Friday morning for the first day of tryouts. If there was a fine line between confidence and cockiness, you might say that his toes may have crossed over into the cocky zone. When he came home he reported that he had done well. Day two proved to be a challenge. His energy level wasn't high enough to keep up with the rigors of the demanding workout. After the practice was over, the coach announced that there would be a list posted on the bulletin board on Monday. The guys were told to check the list and if their names were on it, they were still alive to continue to practice until that Wednesday when final cuts would be announced.

The good news was that his name was on Monday's list. The bad news was that is wasn't on Wednesday's. He was cut. He arrived home, almost in tears, ego shattered and feeling somewhat ashamed that he had probably over evaluated his own ability. As is the case with most kids his age, he wasn't looking forward to school the next day and hearing his non-competing "buddies" give him the business about getting cut.

After dinner, we had a chat. By now he was composed and was probably looking for a little love which is what he got but not what he expected.

"Well, did you play your best?"

"Yes Dad"

"Did you hustle?"

"As best I could. I got tired on the second day and had trouble keeping up. I wasn't in good enough shape".

"It's good you realize that. That issue is easily corrected if you want to. What's next?"

"Play in the town league and try again next season, Is that ok"

"Are you asking what I would do if I were you"?

"Yes"

"Ok, if I were you I would go in tomorrow and see the coach. I would look him in the eye, shake his hand and say, 'Coach,

I'm sorry I didn't impress you enough to make the team this year but I'd like you to tell me what I have to do to improve so I can make it next year." The look he gave me was somewhat like the look you might see on the face of a guy who was about to take his first bungee jump.

The next day he went to school, saw the coach and delivered the message.

The coach said that in all of his coaching years, no kid had ever come to him in such a manner and he admired him for having the character to do so. The coach told him to work on his ball handling, passing and stamina. He then proceeded to work diligently, mostly every day, to improve his skills. He played and did well in the Town League. The coach suggested he attend "unofficial" workouts in the summer. He did some weight training and got stronger. The next year he made the JV team and was moved up to the Varsity. Never the basketball star, his greatest achievements were in the classroom where he excelled throughout high school and college. Recently, he told me that the basketball experience helped him, at that tender age, to realize the true value of hard work and not to take things for granted.

My son is now a husband and father of two young boys. At the appropriate time, I'm sure they will hear how valuable it is to rise above life's little setbacks and turn disappointment into victory.

22

Enjoying the Mystery

ONE OF LIFE'S many mysteries....How can an animal that lives in a dismal environment and eats nothing but the grossest of things taste so good? So is the mystery of the blue claw crab. To me, it's one of the tastiest of God's creations and that would explain the many (and more comical than not) attempts I along with friends and family have made to catch these delicacies.

My first recollection of crabbing was with my father and his cousins in Rhode Island. One of the guys had a little rowboat so we tried our luck in the Narragansett Bay. I was about 5 years old. We used the hand line method, tying a fish head onto a line and dangling it into the water. While holding on to the string, if a crab bit all you had to do was slowly pull the string up and net that sucker. Crabs hate to let go of food once they have begun eating. Unfortunately, we only caught 3 crabs and my father ended up with a deep cut when a hungry flounder yanked the bait so hard that the line cut into his finger which was being used to "feel" for nibbles. Dad needed a couple of stitches.

Flounder 1, Sacchetti's 0.

My next notable experience was with my father, his brother Fred and Grandpop. I was a freshman in college and we went to a "sure fire" spot my uncle found out about near Millville, N.J. A boat was rented for $45.00 for four hours. After one hour we had no bites. I was getting a tad bored so I started singing some pop songs. Uncle Freddy wasn't amused. He told me that I was scaring the crabs away. I said, "What crabs, if there were any around we would have caught one by now". Unimpressed by my logic, he threw a fish head at me, and while looking at my father, said, "Is this kid really in college"? Neither the act of throwing the fish head nor my adept juke to avoid it surprised Grandpop or my Dad. They were blood relatives with many of the same genes.

About a year later, my cousin and I took a trip to Smyrna, Delaware. He heard, from a guy at work, that this was a great place to go so we drove over two hours and rented a boat for

$25.00 It was quite marshy at the dock and we rowed out about 100 yards and dropped our lines. Within 10 minutes we were attacked by a swarm of dreaded "green head" flies, which are famous for their relentless biting of ill prepared city boys. I told my cousin, "Quick, get out the insect repellent." He said, "I thought you brought it." We rowed back in, cut our losses and drove all the way back.

Years later, I took my 5 year old son to Cedar Run, N.J. While working on Rte. 9 at the shore, I noticed a sign that said, "Cedar Run Dock Rd". I figured if it was called Dock Rd., it must lead to a dock. Docks are on the water so let's take a look. It ended up being a good spot. We were able to crab right from the shore. We brought home about 12 "keepers", enough to make a nice pot of crab gravy to be enjoyed with a dish of spaghetti. When we arrived home, my wife set up the pot for us to cook them in but the crabs weren't too happy about the whole idea. In an apparent attempt to run back to the shore, a couple of them jumped out of the bushel basket and onto the kitchen floor. Mother and child ran out of the house screaming leaving good ol' dad to round up the escapees for the inevitable. The gravy was delicious. On a subsequent trip to Cedar run, as we started driving down Dock Rd., I noticed the odometer on my 1978 Chevy Malibu was about to turn 200,000 miles. It was the first car that I had bought brand new. I stopped the car, picked up the little guy and put him on my lap, letting him steer with me. I told him to look at the odometer and take heed because it was very unlikely that he would ever see any American car turn 200,000 miles again.

Several more trips ensued, with my son bringing a buddy or two on more than one occasion. One such trip, when he was about 14, included his best friend. This was his first attempt at crabbing. I brought the video camera for posterity and filmed most of the day. A first, his buddy did an admirable job for a first timer, netting and catching several crabs. He seemed to have a good feel for the line too. If he thought he felt a crab, he was usually right. However, after lunch, he had about 5 "false alarms" in a row, saying he had one when in fact he felt only the tide moving out. This is a common mistake for rookies. We soon dubbed him, "the boy who cried crab", a name he accepted magnanimously. I laugh every time I view the video.

As I look back, I realize that like many events, these crabbing trips were simple treasures that were given to me. Spending time with loved ones and having fun is a true gift. The only investment I made was some time. I'd also like to think that those who accompanied me also received a gift. I know my son did. "The boy who cried crab" was his best man at his wedding. He also remembers the 200,000 mile "turnover" from nearly 30 years ago. Dad and Grandpop enjoyed smoking their pipes and laughing on the boat, despite the attack of the hungry flounder. Uncle Fred realized he had to get his throwing arm in shape, if he ever expected to hit me with a fish head.

Another of life's mysteries…How can the memory of such simple events mean so much and last so long?

23

The 6% Surprise

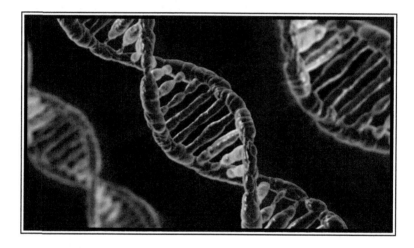

FOR ABOUT 35 years, I have been privileged to make my living in a very interesting way. I have been an outside chemical salesman. Among other things, this requires me to visit a wide range of customers on a monthly basis to service them and help them solve problems. These problems can range from saving rusting equipment, dealing with hydrocarbon spills, cleaning and disinfecting restrooms and melting ice and snow. As you can see, the problems are quite varied. Interestingly, my customers themselves are also quite different in their personalities, likes, dislikes, wants and needs. Interacting with them is what makes the job such a joy because they really aren't customers at all....they are friends who happen to buy things from me.

One such person is my buddy Stan Szczepanek, who recently retired from his position as the man responsible for the operation of a large water facility in the suburbs of Philly. He is a really smart guy and had been my customer for 26 years. I truly treasured my monthly visits. The real fun in seeing Stan was not making the sale, although I thoroughly enjoyed that but the banter and exchanging of life experiences. One such experience, related to me over the years, was his progress in developing his "family tree". To date it has been an 8 year effort and he has successfully found relatives dating back to the 1500's. Along the way he decided to include something, in his arsenal, that he has had an interest in for many years.

The concept of DNA and its potential to unlock various secrets seemed a perfect tool to use as he continued his investigation. He explained to me how DNA could give a reliable indication of one's ancestry since groups of people tended to settle and live in specific areas. When a large data base is used to map out the similarities in the DNA, one could get a very accurate idea of where his ancestors came from hence his ethnicity. The concept was intriguing.

With each monthly visit I would toy with the idea of taking the DNA test myself, just for the fun of it. Who knows, maybe I was a descendant of Leonardo Da Vinci or the great-great-great-great grandson of the guy who invented pizza! What a feather in my cap that would be! So, I decided to spring for the $99.00 and take the test. I received my kit from "Ancestry DNA" and I was off and running. The whole process was very simple. All I had to do was fill a small test tube with my saliva, cork it and mail it to the lab in the neat little box they provided, postage paid and all. The tube already had my control code number on it so I couldn't be confused with some 6' 4" Swede if he decided to take the plunge. They promised to have the results back in two weeks. I received periodic updates via e mail and after about two weeks I received the e mail that said:

"Great news! Your AncestryDNA™ results are in."

Ok, let's get to the results!

I clicked on the "Ethnicity Estimate" link to see what I was made of, so to speak. The results were somewhat interesting:

72% Italy/Greece....no surprise there. This is a very high percentage based on the data base.

22% Middle East...including places like Lebanon, Turkey, and Jordan. No big surprise here either. These places are just a hop, skip and a swim across the Mediterranean.

And then:

6% European Jew...This was interesting news. It all made sense to me now. I've always loved corned beef on rye, chopped liver and matzo ball soup.

So what do you think I did after I found out this revelation? I have a dear friend, Arnie Bromberg, who happens to be an 87 year old Jewish man who was one of my mentors in the chemical business. Arnie, a man's man, still works every day and covers some of the toughest areas of New York. He's the kind of guy who can size you up in 5 minutes and decide whether he likes you or not. If he does, you have friend for life. If not, don't let the door hit you on the way out. Luckily for me, I had a good 5 minutes and we have been friends for 35 years. He has always had an affinity for Italians and our culture although he rarely resists the opportunity to tease me about all of our foods, customs and holy feast days. I always repaid the friendly barbs with vigor. So at 8 p.m. the following night I picked up the phone to give him a call...

"How ya doin', Arnie boy"?

"Ok what's up kid"?

I then explained that I took the DNA test and got the results:

"Now I know why you love me so much"

"Why"

"Because I'm 6% Jewish. I'm just like you"

After a hearty laugh and a "welcome to the club" he said,

"Well how does it feel to be a Jew"

"Well Arn, I can't really say but when I woke up this morning I had an uncontrollable urge to go out and buy a building."

He laughed so hard he dropped the phone.

Of course, I'm sure this bit of news will not change me in the least. After all, I'm 69 years old and pretty set in my ways. I'd better close now. I feel like I'm coming down with a cold. I think I'll go get some chicken soup.

God bless you all!

24

When an Impulse Pays Off

IN THE FALL of 2012, I saw the promo on PBS and it looked pretty interesting. It was for an upcoming documentary, **"Paesani: Italian Culture in Northeast Pennsylvania"** which would air on Saturday evening. Being a grandson of 4 Italian immigrants, I naturally had an interest in the subject so I decided to give it a shot. The program was a joy! It showed how a large group of Italians settled in the area around Scranton, PA. mostly, during the 1920's. It documented the hardships the people suffered, coming over in large, crowded, aged boats with the hope of finding a better life for their families. The documentary was done in a style that included numerous interviews of people, most now elderly, who either came over themselves as children or had parents who did so. They related their personal stories of good and bad times in a way that made you feel you went through it with them. It showed how the people brought their culture with them regarding food, religion and lifestyle but always knowing that they were now proud Americans. In particular, one such interviewee caught my eye and in doing so he gave me an opportunity to experience some of the most delightful times of my life.

Al Pisa was in his 80's when he appeared on the show from his home in the "Bunker Hill" section of Dunmore, PA. As soon as I saw and heard him I thought of my father's beloved cousin, Frank Fusco, who passed away years ago at his home in Warwick, Rhode Island. Like Frank, Al's personality filled the room. His stories about his family experiences were told in a way that grabbed your attention and simply made you smile. When he spoke of his family, you could see the warmth and the light of his heart shine through. His wife Angie and son Carlo were also featured in the show. Carlo gave a succinct account of how his Bunker Hill neighbors all essentially came from the same mountain village in Italy, Guardia dei Lombardi. They were friends and family over there and now they were friends and family over here.

The next day, my wife and I returned from breakfast after Sunday mass. Still thinking of how much I loved the Paesani documentary, on an impulse, I decided to tell Al Pisa how much I enjoyed him on the show. I reasoned, how many 80 year old Al Pisa's can there be in Dunmore, PA? I should be able to find Al by doing a "people search" on the computer." So, at 11:00 a.m. I Googled "Al Pisa, Dunmore, PA". The first listing showed Al Pisa, age 85! I called the number and a lady answered. "Hello is this Angie?" "Yes" she said "who is this?" I explained I was just an Italian guy from Jersey who saw the show last night and just wanted to tell Al how much I enjoyed him and his story telling. "Oh, ok hold on." Al greeted me with a big hello and we had a 30 minute conversation that covered everything from his resembling my cousin to why he called it "sauce" instead of "gravy." The conversation ended with me telling him that Robert DeNiro better watch out because Al Pisa was on a roll and probably would become the next box office attraction. He finished by making me promise that I'd come up to see him and after doing so, we said goodbye. Five minutes later, my phone rang and the caller ID said "Al Pisa" so I answered it and said "What's up Al"? The caller said, "No this isn't Al, it's his son Carlo. I just wanted to thank you for calling. You made my father's day." I told Carlo I'd be in touch and we would all arrange to have lunch in Scranton.

By now it was the next year. Al's family and mine had exchanged Christmas cards in December and being late May, it was a good time to make the arrangements to go up to see the Pisa's. I called Carlo, said hello and was greeted with a silent moment that was instantly troubling. Al had passed away, just weeks before and the family was grieving. After some words of comfort, I told Carlo that I still intended to honor my promise to Al and we made a date to get together.

My friend, Bill Winarski and I made the trip to Dunmore and had a wonderful lunch with Carlo and Angie at a local Italian (what else) restaurant. He took us to see his buddies who were volunteering their time doing maintenance at St. Rocco's church and the whole visit was like spending time with your beloved family. Carlo told me about a tradition Al had each fall. He would host a Bocce Tournament for his friends at his house. This was a tradition that had gone on for years and Carlo invited Bill and me to come back in the fall to attend. We did so and boy did we have a ball!

Adjacent to the Bocce court was the gathering area. We enjoyed the food presented on a table under the large grape vine including but not limited to salami, prosciutto, various cheeses, hot and sweet peppers, tomatoes, egg plant and crusty Italian bread. The layout rivaled the quality of hors d'oeuvres you would hope for at a traditional Italian wedding. After hours of food, wine, laughs, hugs and bocce (rules made up as you go) we sat down to a dinner fit for an Italian cruise ship. The meal was blessed by the local parish priest and ended with an incredible pastry display provided by Dave "the Mailman" Evanko. Dave makes his living as a mailman but his passion is baking. Words can't describe his talent.

Bill and I, dubbed "The Jersey Boys", will be making our fourth annual trip up there this fall to attend what is now called the "Al Pisa Memorial Bocce Tournament." Carlo, his son Alfredo, Dave the Mailman and about 25 other guys have become cherished friends and it feels as though I have known them all of my life.

Thank God I picked up the phone on that Sunday to place that call. The result has enriched my life. And God bless Al who I know has orchestrated every move.

25

A Good Memory at a Tough Time

AT THE AGE of 15, I had somewhat of a "crisis" to deal with. In the spring of 1962 I found out that the baseball team, that I had played for, was breaking up and I had become a young "free agent." Our manager simply had too many family commitments and couldn't devote the time necessary to run the team. I immediately started to consider which other team, in the neighborhood, I would like to join.

Across the street lived an older kid who was a very good player for West Catholic High and also our local American Legion team, the William P. Roche Post #21. The league was for 16-18 year olds, most of the guys being local high school players. The season started after school was dismissed for summer vacation. I knew the legion team had an exhibition game that Saturday afternoon, so I decided to take the mile or so walk to 58th and Elmwood Ave. to watch him play. In the stands I saw his father, who was relaxing and getting ready to see his kid's team take the field, so I strolled over and sat with him. In about the third inning, he asked me where I was playing this summer. I explained that I didn't know and related the circumstances. Saying nothing more, he immediately got up and walked behind the batting cage, to the manager of the team. A minute or two later, that manager, John Hayes, waved while beckoning me to come over to him. John said, "This gentleman tells me you're a good player with no team." When I confirmed it he said, "Good, I want you to hit next inning." Now, there I stood, dressed in shorts, tee shirt and my low cut black Converse Chuck Taylor all stars. Of course, every other kid on the field was dressed in their spiffy baseball uniforms and spiked shoes. When I stepped to the plate to hit, there were more than a few snickers and giggles but they abruptly ended when I lined the 2nd pitch to right center. As I rounded first base, slipping and sliding (Sneakers are not the preferred footwear on a baseball field) the first base coach said, "go, go!" I made it to third base with a stand-up triple. John Hayes, who was coaching third base said, "Welcome to the team." I played for him for 4 years.

After that, playing college ball and going away in the summers to play, I lost contact with John until 40 years later when Jimmy Stuffo, a friend of mine, met John at a New Year's Eve party. They started talking baseball and somehow my name came up. Jimmy called me at home and turned the phone over to John. It was a great reunion. I arranged to take John and his wife, Marie to lunch shortly thereafter. We continued to stay in touch with an occasional lunch or phone call. Then one day, I found out that John was seriously ill.

During his courageous fight, I gathered up a couple of my teammates, John's old players and we had several nice visits. He pulled out some old pictures of his teams and we reminisced with the camaraderie only soldiers and teammates can understand. The thing I remember most was our first visit when John, in obvious pain, stopped in the middle of flipping through the pictures and asked me, "Do you remember the first hit you ever got for me"? Of course, it was so dramatic that I could never forget it but I was amazed that he held that moment in his mind for nearly 50 years. When we rehashed the story of the kid slipping and sliding on the way to third base, I saw a smile on his face that made him forget the pain for an instant.

Seeing him smile only made me happier that he asked me to grab that bat back in the spring of 1962.

26

No Harm in Asking

MY FATHER, HENRY, paid a price for working at the Westinghouse Plant in Lester, PA for 40 plus years. The constant pounding of his "Drop Forge Hammer" had caused him to lose most of his hearing. He was "old school" and happy to have this job that kept my mother and him fed and warm during their 65 year marriage. Suing the company was out of the question for a man like him. He knew the risks and that was that. My mother, sister and I got used to having to elevate our voices when we spoke with Dad. We also got used to the TV blaring at night and my Buist Ave. neighbors enjoyed the free radio broadcasts of every Phillies game that emanated each summer from the open screened windows. My dear friend Tom Manieri, who was a member of the wonderful service organization The Lion's Club, used his influence to provide Dad with two free hearing aids. The only problem was that Dad didn't like them so he rarely used them. Also, typically with most hard of hearing people, he tended to speak in a very loud voice so that he could hear himself!

As he grew older, he developed some health problems. He became an insulin dependent diabetic. Well into his 80's and a widower after Mom's death, he valued his independence and was quite self sufficient. He was still driving at age 87. I kept close tabs on him and came to realize that the effects of the diabetes were becoming dangerous. We had discussed the possibility of giving up his car, which he staunchly resisted.

Until one night.

At the dinner table, his sugar level dropped and he was "out of it" for about 20 seconds. After I said that being out of control for that long while driving, could possibly cause an accident and might result in an innocent kid's death, he agreed right then and there to stop driving. I took the keys, gave them to my cousin and Dad's driving days were over. A result of this was that now it was my responsibility to take him wherever he had to go, whether it be shopping, to the doctor's, to visit his sister and yes, even to church every Sunday unless my niece, his granddaughter, would pay a visit. I didn't mind. It gave us a chance to get together and talk about family and baseball, his two favorite topics.

Dad and Mom belonged to Our Lady of Loreto church, located at 62nd and Grays Ave in Southwest Philly. This was one of the old ethnic parishes and the parishioners were mostly Italian Americans. My parents had been fixtures at 8 o'clock mass every Sunday for over 50 years, occupying the same seats in the second row just to the right of the speaker's podium. With Mom gone, I would pick up Dad, sit in those same seats and since no one sat in the front row, we were the closest parishioners to the priest.

Dad was now 90 years old and on one particular Sunday, we had a young visiting priest. He was sent by the bishop to share his experiences during his six months of studies in Rome. As the guest started to give his remarks, our pastor took his seat, just to our left. Our guest was an enthusiastic young man but to say that he was a bit "wordy" would be an understatement. First he spoke for a few minutes of the overall beauty of Rome. He then gave his impressions of Vatican City, which included a 10 minute description of the Sistine Chapel that the most seasoned tour guide would envy. This was followed by another 10 minutes or so of his thoughts of St. Peter's Basilica, the Coliseum and the Apian Way. I felt as though I'd soon be hearing the banging of heads on the wooden pews, as the congregation fell asleep one by one. Remarkably, my father just sat there, wide awake, watching the young man speak. All of a sudden he turned to me and said in a very audible voice,

"What's this guy talking about?"

Our guest's eyes opened wide. I looked for a place to hide but alas there was none. Our pastor smiled perhaps giving tacit approval. Dad just sat there without having his question answered.

After mass, as we filed out, a couple of the old Italian guys in the congregation came up to us and patted Dad on the back. One man said, he wished he had asked that question. Dad didn't mean to be disrespectful. He would never do that. However, I think his easily overheard question served two purposes. The first is that the young priest must have realized he had gone on too long and was losing his audience. He ended his talk soon after Dad's question. The second is that perhaps the young priest learned a lesson in brevity and hopefully this would help him in years to come as he tended to his flock.

27

What a Gal

RECENTLY MY DEAR friend, Carol Salinsky, lost her mother, Ruth. By all accounts, she was a wonderful woman who raised a great family. In sympathizing with my friend, I was led to reflect on my own mother, Catherine's, passing back in 2002. It seems no matter how old we are we're only kids in grown up bodies and the memories flow freely........

"Kate" was a "housewife." Back in the 1950's few mothers worked outside of the home. Mom was a 5'1" Sicilian bundle of energy that ran the house, paid the bills, did the cooking, and protected her two kids like a mama bear protects her cubs. She was at once tender and ferocious, always there to give a hug when needed or bandage a cut but woe to the unsuspecting neighborhood huckster who tried to overcharge her for three pounds of Jersey tomatoes.

I remember the time when I was about 7 years old and just starting to be a little "pesky." We had a peddler in the neighborhood, known as "Joe Bananas." Joe used to come by periodically to try to sell whatever he had gotten his hands on. Watching him try to sell Mom something was more fun than watching the Little Rascals. One day he came by with a new vacuum cleaner. As luck would have it ours had just broken so Mom consented to let him do a demo. He sprinkled some confetti on the floor and the machine only picked up about 1/3 of it. Saying only what I guessed Mom to be thinking, I said, "That's a piece of junk." Joe looked at me and said, "Look kid, nobody likes a wise guy". Saying nothing, Mom grabbed me by the arm and led me into the kitchen. "Charlie, don't you give him a hard time, that's my job."

We had the old vacuum repaired.

Dad would work his job at Westinghouse and bring home his weekly pay check. After Dad took expense money, Mom would do her magician act and pay all of the bills, buy all of the food, clothes or whatever else we needed. In fact, she even could find a way to put a few bucks away in case we needed some cash down the line. We always had food, clothes and a warm house because Mom was a master at stretching a dollar.

Mom had a healthy streak of vanity and was always conscious of the way she looked. The one luxury she allowed herself, was a weekly Friday morning trip to the hairdresser. These trips were usually fully funded from her bingo winnings as she attended games, a couple of nights a week, at local churches. When she would leave the house to walk to the game, Dad would say, "There goes Mom off to work!"

Mom was born in April, Dad in August. My sister, Kathy, Dad and I always assumed and Mom never corrected our belief that she was 4 months older than Dad. When it was time for Dad to sign up for Social Security he naturally had Mom do likewise. At that point the big secret was revealed that Mom was in fact, 5 years older than Dad. She just didn't want to let anyone know how old she was. Dad's reaction…"Who cares? We're married 40 years, big deal". Mom's guarding of her age, to others, lasted until she became 80. She looked so good that she would ask strangers, like waitresses, how old they thought she was. When they said, 65, Mom gleefully revealed her actual age, as if it were a badge of honor. She would always say that, "I don't feel old, I'm young at heart", an obvious reference to her favorite Sinatra song.

April 26, 2002 was a Friday and 4 days after Mom's 94th birthday. After visiting a customer, I decided to give Mom and Dad a call to see how things were going. When Dad answered the phone I heard the worry in his voice as he said, "I think Mom is having a stroke!" He had just driven her back from her hairdresser appointment and was outside tending to his flowers while Mom went in to make lunch. When he came into the house, not seeing Mom in the kitchen, he went in to find her on the floor, just as I called. I told him to quick call 911 which he did. Mom was taken to the University of Pennsylvania hospital. The fact that she arrived just 20 minutes after the onset of the stroke gave her a 50-50 chance of having successful surgery and possibly recovering. However, it was not to be and two weeks later, the night before Mother's day on May 11th, Mom passed away. It was on that day that Dad told me that as the EMT's were picking Mom up to put her on the gurney, she told them she first had to finish making Dad's lunch.

No one, in the family, was surprised.